POINTS OF VIEW

Should the SCHOOL DAY Start Later?

By Riley Lawrence

Published in 2020 by
KidHaven Publishing, an Imprint of Greenhaven Publishing, LLC
353 3rd Avenue
Suite 255
New York, NY 10010

Copyright © 2020 KidHaven Publishing, an Imprint of Greenhaven Publishing, LLC.

All rights reserved. No part of this book may be reproduced in any form without permission in writing from the publisher, except by a reviewer.

Designer: Deanna Paternostro
Editor: Katie Kawa

Photo credits: Cover wavebreakmedia/Shutterstock.com; p. 5 (top) SaMBa/Shutterstock.com; p. 5 (bottom) Syda Productions/Shutterstock.com; p. 7 (top-left) Alfaguarilla/Shutterstock.com; pp. 7 (top-right), 21 (inset, middle-left) Monkey Business Images/Shutterstock.com; pp. 7 (bottom-left), 21 (inset, right) Africa Studio/Shutterstock.com; p. 7 (bottom-right) My Life Graphic/Shutterstock.com; p. 9 Oleg Golovnev/Shutterstock.com; p. 11 Dragon Images/Shutterstock.com; p. 13 sebra/Shutterstock.com; p. 15 mTaira/Shutterstock.com; p. 17 Lisa F. Young/Shutterstock.com; p. 19 Ariel Skelley/DigitalVision/Getty Images; p. 21 (notepad) ESB Professional/Shutterstock.com; p. 21 (markers) Kucher Serhii/Shutterstock.com; p. 21 (photo frame) FARBAI/iStock/Thinkstock; p. 21 (inset, left) Mladen Zivkovic/Shutterstock.com; p. 21 (inset, middle-right) Rido/Shutterstock.com.

Cataloging-in-Publication Data

Names: Lawrence, Riley.
Title: Should the school day start later? / Riley Lawrence.
Description: New York : KidHaven Publishing, 2020. | Series: Points of view | Includes glossary and index.
Identifiers: ISBN 9781534529908 (pbk.) | ISBN 9781534567207 (library bound) | ISBN 9781534531178 (6 pack) | ISBN 9781534529915 (ebook)
Subjects: LCSH: Education–United States–Juvenile literature. | Children–Sleep–Juvenile literature. | Sleep–Physiological aspects–Juvenile literature.
Classification: LCC LB1556.L39 2020 | DDC 370–dc23

Printed in the United States of America

CPSIA compliance information: Batch #BS19KL: For further information contact Greenhaven Publishing LLC, New York, New York at 1-844-317-7404.

Please visit our website, www.greenhavenpublishing.com. For a free color catalog of all our high-quality books, call toll free 1-844-317-7404 or fax 1-844-317-7405.

CONTENTS

School or Sleep?	4
Sleepy Students	6
Changing Bodies	8
The Elementary Effect	10
In the Classroom	12
What Happens After School?	14
Safety First!	16
Problems for Parents	18
Listening and Learning	20
Glossary	22
For More Information	23
Index	24

School or SLEEP?

What time do you wake up to go to school? Many students wake up early in the morning to get to class on time. Some people believe this is a **normal** part of growing up. However, other people believe the school day starts too early. They feel students would be healthier and do better on tests if they could sleep in later.

It's important for students to form and share opinions on issues that directly **affect** them, such as when to start the school day. Read on to learn the facts about this **debate** before you take a side!

Know the Facts!

A 2014 study showed that more than 80 percent of middle schools in the United States started classes before 8:30 a.m.

It's easy to say that you think the school day should start later because you don't like getting up early. However, that's not an informed, or educated, opinion. An informed opinion is supported by facts.

Sleepy STUDENTS

The debate about when to start the school day is often in the news. This is because doctors think students aren't getting enough sleep, and one way to fix that is to start the school day later.

In 2016, doctors who study sleep stated that children between the ages of 6 and 12 should sleep for at least 9 hours every night. They also stated that teenagers should sleep for at least 8 hours every night. However, most teenagers are getting less than that amount of sleep. This can be bad for their health.

Know the Facts!

A major study on teenagers and sleep was done in 2013. This study found that around 69 percent of high school students slept for less than 8 hours on school nights.

Turning off smartphones and other **devices** 30 minutes before bedtime, cutting down on watching TV at night, and giving students less homework can help young people get enough sleep. Many doctors also believe starting the school day later can help with this problem.

Changing BODIES

If kids need more sleep, why don't they just go to bed earlier? This is a question many people ask, but doctors believe it's not quite that simple—especially for teenagers.

Teenagers get tired later than they did when they were younger. This is because their bodies are going through many changes that make it hard for them to fall asleep at an earlier time. They need to sleep in later in the morning to make up for this change. However, they can't sleep in on a school day unless classes start later.

Know the Facts!

Doctors have stated that getting enough sleep is very important for a healthy body and mind. Certain health problems, such as **depression**, are more common in people who don't get enough sleep.

It's hard to fall asleep when you're not tired, and teenagers get tired later than they used to. This is why many teenagers like to sleep in when they can.

The Elementary EFFECT

Many people believe starting the school day later could help older students in middle school and high school. However, there are more debates about its effect on younger students.

If the school day starts later at middle schools and high schools, it would most likely need to start later at elementary schools, too. However, younger students get tired earlier than teenagers. If their school day started later, they would have a greater chance of being tired at the end of the school day. They might even fall asleep on the bus ride home and miss their stop!

Know the Facts!

In many U.S. school districts, or groups of schools, elementary schools start their school day later than middle schools and high schools.

Some teachers have reported that elementary students have a harder time paying attention in class when the school day starts later.

In the CLASSROOM

When students are tired, their grades suffer. They have a hard time **focusing** on tasks and remembering facts for tests. If the school day started later, students would be able to get more rest. This could help raise their grades and improve their test scores.

Some school districts that have moved to a later start time have seen a rise in attendance, too. Students are more likely to come to school if they got enough sleep the night before. Starting the school day later can also help more students get to school on time instead of being late.

Know the Facts!

A group of U.S. doctors who work with children stated that all middle schools and high schools should start their school day at 8:30 a.m. or later.

When students oversleep and miss time in class, they miss learning important things.

What Happens After SCHOOL?

Although starting the school day later might be better for students' grades, some people believe it's not good for students' lives outside the classroom. Ending the school day later gives students less time to take part in after-school activities. Games for sports teams and meetings for clubs would have to take place later. This would be hard for younger students, who get tired earlier than older students.

Many high school students also have after-school jobs. A later school day would make it harder for them to work, do their homework, and get enough sleep.

Know the Facts!

A 2014 report showed that 57 percent of children between the ages of 6 and 17 took part in at least one after-school activity. Playing a sport was the most common thing these children did after school.

After-school activities are an important part of many students' lives, but starting the school day later gives them less time to take part in things such as sports or music lessons.

Safety FIRST!

It can be hard to balance a later school day with other activities, but many people believe it's worth it. One of the biggest reasons they feel this way is because starting the school day later has been shown to keep students—especially teenagers—safer.

Some teenagers drive themselves to school. When teenagers are tired or rushing to get to school on time, they have a greater chance of being in a car crash. A later start to the school day has been shown in some studies to lower the number of car crashes among teenage drivers.

Know the Facts!

Doctors have stated that young people who don't get enough sleep are more likely to do dangerous, or unsafe, things such as using illegal drugs.

It's important for teenagers to always be as safe as possible in a car. This includes only driving when they've had enough sleep and never getting in a car with someone who seems too tired to drive.

Problems for PARENTS

Most students don't drive themselves to school. This becomes a problem when the school day starts later. School buses run on set **schedules**, and these can be hard to change for a later start time. In addition, some students are dropped off at school by their parents on their way to work. If the school day starts later, these parents could then be late for work.

Some older students babysit their younger siblings after school. They wouldn't be able to do this if they were in school later in the day. Instead, their parents would have to find someone else to watch them.

Know the Facts!

In a 2017 study, 49 percent of parents said they thought it was a bad idea to start the school day later than 8:30 a.m. for high school students.

Even if the school day starts later, some parents still need to drop their children off at school early to get to work on time.

19

Listening and
LEARNING

School districts are using these different opinions about the start of the school day to make big decisions about their schedules. They often hold meetings where parents, teachers, school officials, and students share their opinions before any decisions are made. These meetings often feature respectful debates where people can learn about different points of view. In some cases, people are able to vote for what start time they think is best for students.

After learning about both sides of this debate, do you think the school day should start later? What facts can you use to support your opinion?

Know the Facts!

In 2017, the first state bill about school start times was **introduced** by California lawmakers. It stated that all public middle schools and high schools would be required to start the school day at 8:30 a.m. or later.

Should the school day start later?

YES

- Teenagers aren't getting enough sleep, and their changing bodies are built to fall asleep later and wake up later.

- Starting the school day later has led to better grades and attendance for students.

- When teenage drivers get more rest and don't have to rush to school, they lower their chance of getting in a car crash.

NO

- Starting school later also affects elementary students, who get tired when the school day runs later.

- A later school day would cut down on time for after-school activities and jobs.

- It can be hard for working parents to get their children to school at a later time or find childcare for younger children when older children are at school later.

> You can use a chart such as this one to remember the most important arguments and facts on both sides of a debate. This can make it easier for you to form your own opinion on issues that matter to you.

GLOSSARY

affect: To produce an effect on something.

debate: An argument or discussion about an issue, generally between two sides.

depression: A medical condition in which a person feels very sad and hopeless and is not interested in things they once enjoyed.

device: A tool used for a certain purpose.

focus: To direct attention or effort at something.

introduce: To bring forward to be considered or talked about.

normal: Usual.

schedule: A list of times when certain events will happen.

For More INFORMATION

WEBSITES

KidsHealth: "Why Do I Need Sleep?"
kidshealth.org/en/kids/sleep.html
This article from the KidsHealth website features facts about sleep and a game kids can play about how much sleep different living things need.

Sleep for Kids
www.sleepforkids.org
The National Sleep Foundation created this website to help kids understand the importance of sleep by using fun facts and games.

BOOKS

Lamothe, Matt. *This Is How We Do It: One Day in the Lives of Seven Kids from Around the World.* San Francisco, CA: Chronicle Books, 2017.

Marsico, Katie. *Get a Good Night's Sleep!* Ann Arbor, MI: Cherry Lake Publishing, 2015.

Salzmann, Mary Elizabeth. *Sleep All Night!: Healthy Sleeping Habits.* Minneapolis, MN: Sandcastle, 2015.

Publisher's note to educators and parents: Our editors have carefully reviewed these websites to ensure that they are suitable for students. Many websites change frequently, however, and we cannot guarantee that a site's future contents will continue to meet our high standards of quality and educational value. Be advised that students should be closely supervised whenever they access the Internet.

INDEX

A
after-school activities, 14, 15, 21

B
babysitting, 18

C
California, 20
car crashes, 16, 21

D
doctors, 6, 7, 8, 12, 16

E
elementary schools, 10, 11, 21

H
health problems, 8
high schools, 6, 10, 12, 14, 18, 20
homework, 7, 14

J
jobs, 14, 18, 19, 21

M
meetings, 14, 20
middle schools, 4, 10, 12, 20

O
oversleeping, 13

S
schedules, 18, 20
school districts, 10, 12, 20
smartphones, 7
sports, 14, 15

T
teachers, 11, 20
teenagers, 6, 8, 9, 10, 16, 17, 21
tests, 4, 12